Quite Early One Planet

the arrival

Brilliant Books Literary
137 Forest Park Lane Thomasville
North Carolina 27360 USA

Quite Early One Planet

the arrival

a living alphabet arrives on planet earth

jerome austin mcnicholl

Dedication:
For the 'glow' in everyone's shadow, may they find it-
listen to its whispers.

"In the beginning, all knowledge and wisdom were with the animals".

Joseph Campbell

Long after light
gave birth to our planet
after the seas
gave creatures to the land
there hovered in spirit
upon our earth home
a great 'Weaver of Words'.

The Weaver waited...
when two of earth's creatures
stepped forward to find
they had minds,
the Weaver sent a gift.

8

9

THE GIFT

To create words
an alphabet there must be...

and for this, you need an A to lead.

Before alphabets and long before words
Argo a dust frog was born to Gunallia and Bodinga
two warm hearted landbound frogs.
One night near their little coastal home
by the Newtonian sea they were devoured
by giant stinger star fish.

Argo escapes. Filled with fear and terror, he headed
inland, with only one purpose
to find a safe place to be.

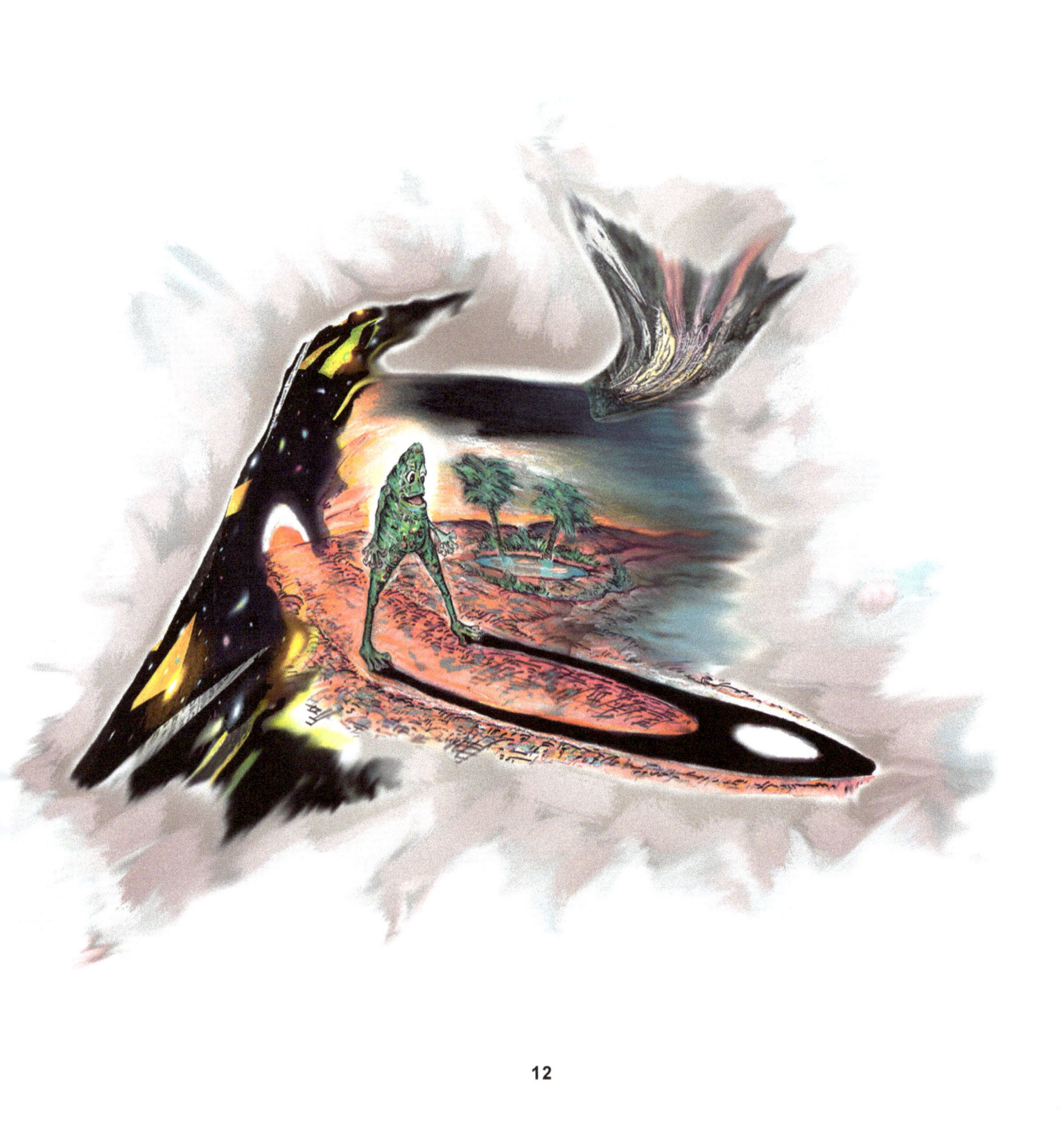

On a sea of sand Argo
found refuge in a desert land.
As the years inched away
the fear and terror of life
by the Newtonian sea fadded:
he grew tired of being alone,
and longed to find other's like himself

One day at sundown his shadow
stretched out before him, in it was a glow.

From within the glow,
a voice whispered,
"Argo, find your B, C, and D
all of the others will follow...
you will know them when you see them
and they you...you my dear friend
will become an A,"

The 'glow'
in Argo's shadow
gave him hope.

He knew not why,
but he needed
B, C, D
and who ever the 'other's
might be.

 nervous and afraid
Argo tried to be brave
as he set out to find
what the voice in his shadow
had in mind.

Argo stumbled into a world
strange and cruel...
a gentle turtel told him "keep on the move...
to the north there is a passage, take it.

The one's you seek are arriving now
on planet earth
from all parts of the universe."

When Argo emerged from his dark night...
he saw that the nameless turtle had been right.

The creatures born of the Weavers mind,
each one unique and kind
are coming into sight.

by two's, three's,
sixfold and five
they arrived.

"You will know them
when you see them
and they you."

20

The creatures
to become X and Z
Argo had never
seen before

From out of nowhere
arrived the gift
of W and I.

Earth and the cosmos dreamed their dreams, bringing forth
the creatures soon to become B C and D

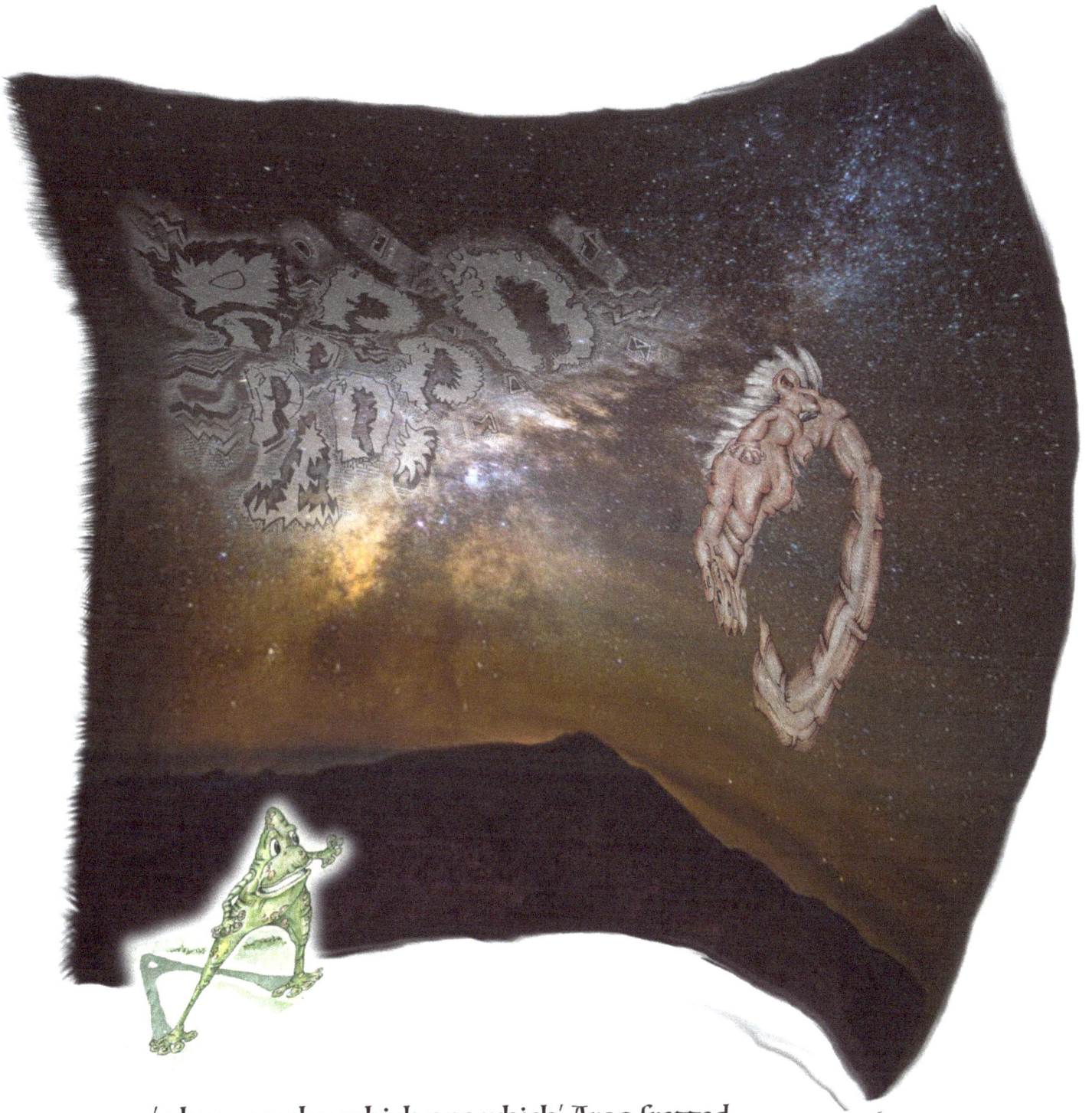

'who was who, which one which' Argo fretted.

The Weaver
wove in silence
each creature to be unique
bathed them in pools of time
morning, noon and night...
thus T, S, and U
came to life

The alchemy
of the Weavers art
is sometimes strange,
often elusive but never intrusive.

Each creature had to find it's own path,
some were uneasy, only a few knew the way,

29

Gaseous clouds
endless nights
rivers of darkness,
atoms
of
light...

...brought forth
J and E

By the winds
of father sky
to mother earth
they came,
each one ready
to meet
the others.

The creature to become the R
guided the final four
to the gathering place
where they all will meet.

Everyone stood perfectly still
as Argo climed a small hill,
his shadow stretching out
before him...in it
was the
'glow'.

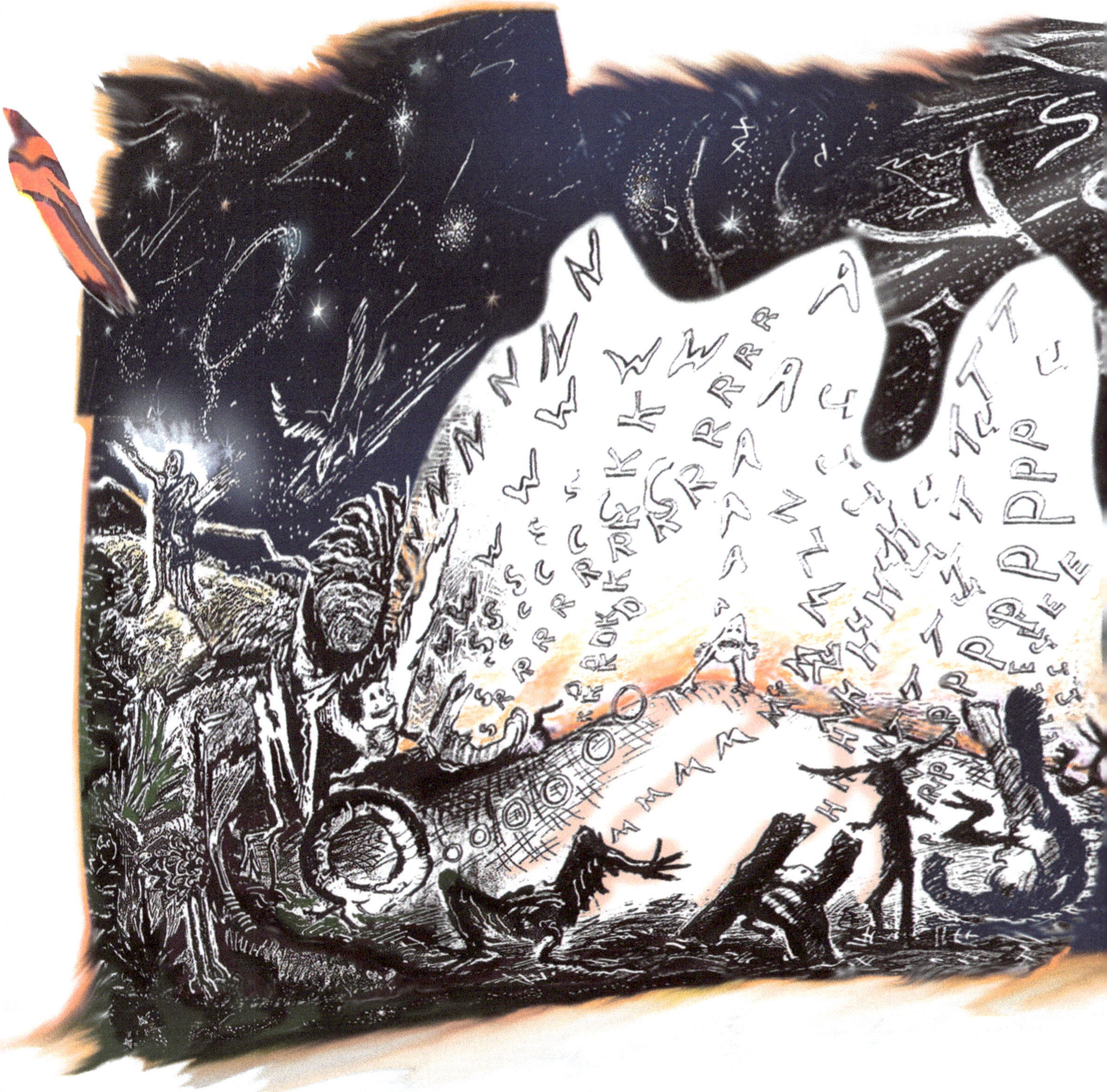

At that moment
each creature felt their 'glow'.
They sang and danced
round and round
each to the music
of their own
letter sound.

Like bird song
from morning to night
their letter sounds
took flight...
all around the earth.

When morning light
gathered everyone around
the Weavers gift
was nearly
complete.

The creature
to become the T
stepped forward
to recieve Argo

"All of us here have come
from far and wide
to become with you
a part of something special,"
her face full with delight
as were all the others

"each of us carries a wish...
to be a part of
the Weavers gift".

The Weaver whispered to each one
"You will travel to the humans
make yourselves seen and heard
so the humans can learn
to make Words,

you my dear friends
are an Alphabet...

this you must never forget."

From scribble to alphabets
the human's went
helped by the creatures the Weaver had sent.
In time humans learned to make words
with unusual sounds
and lively verbs.

Little by little
humans found their glow,
better coming to know
each other...
and the infinite universe
that embraces
them
all.

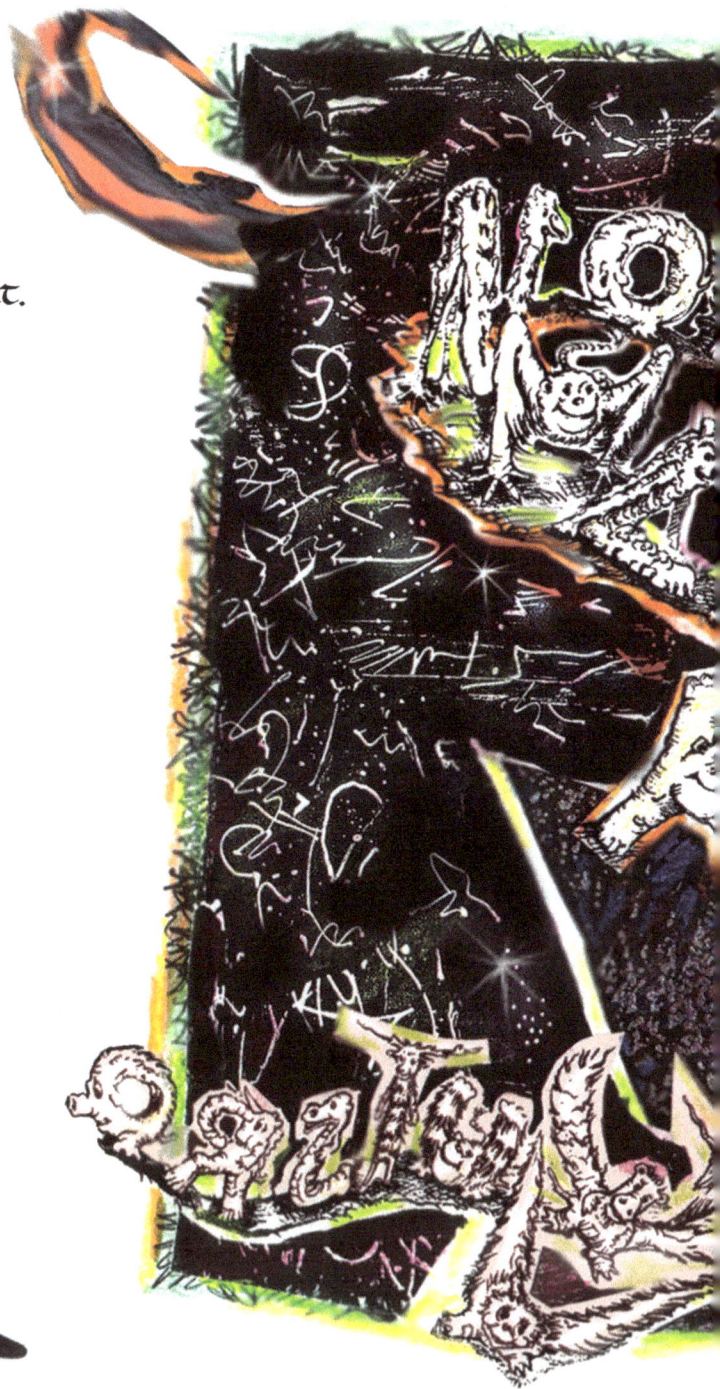

Hey - find a pencil
or a pen,
ruler
+ cutting tool

you can have this
Alphabet
on
your
wall...

so cool.

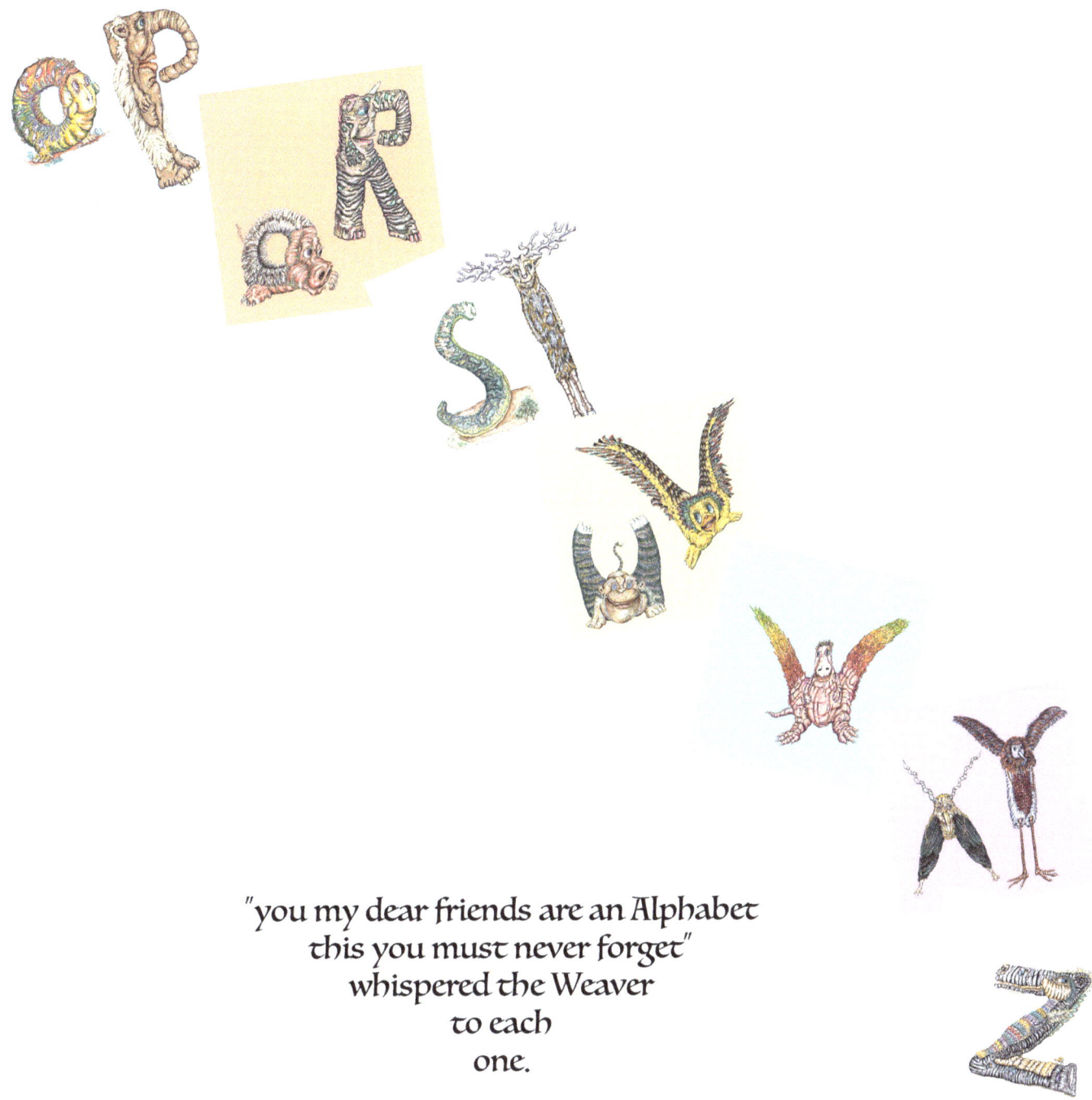

"you my dear friends are an Alphabet
this you must never forget"
whispered the Weaver
to each
one.

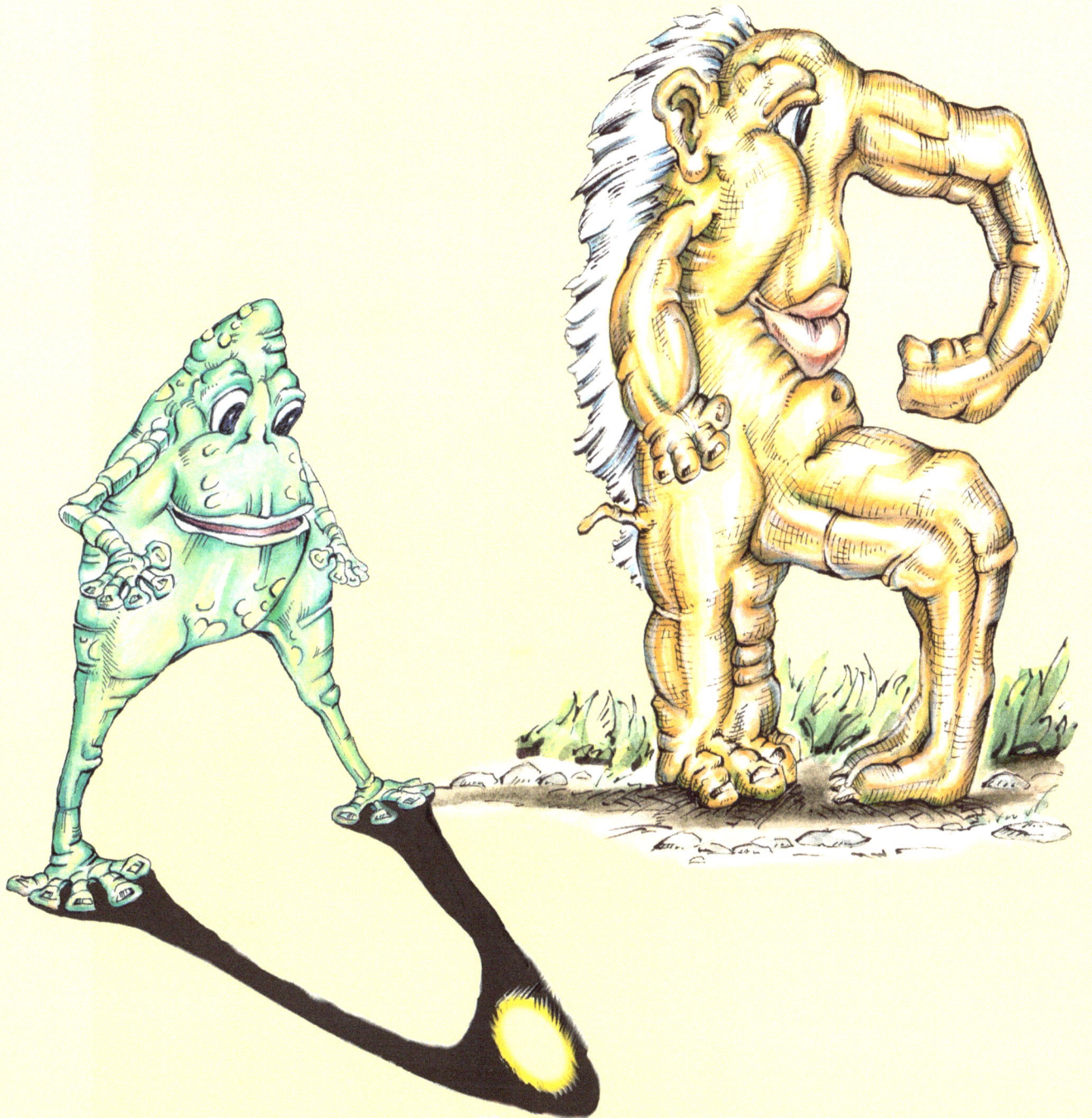

49

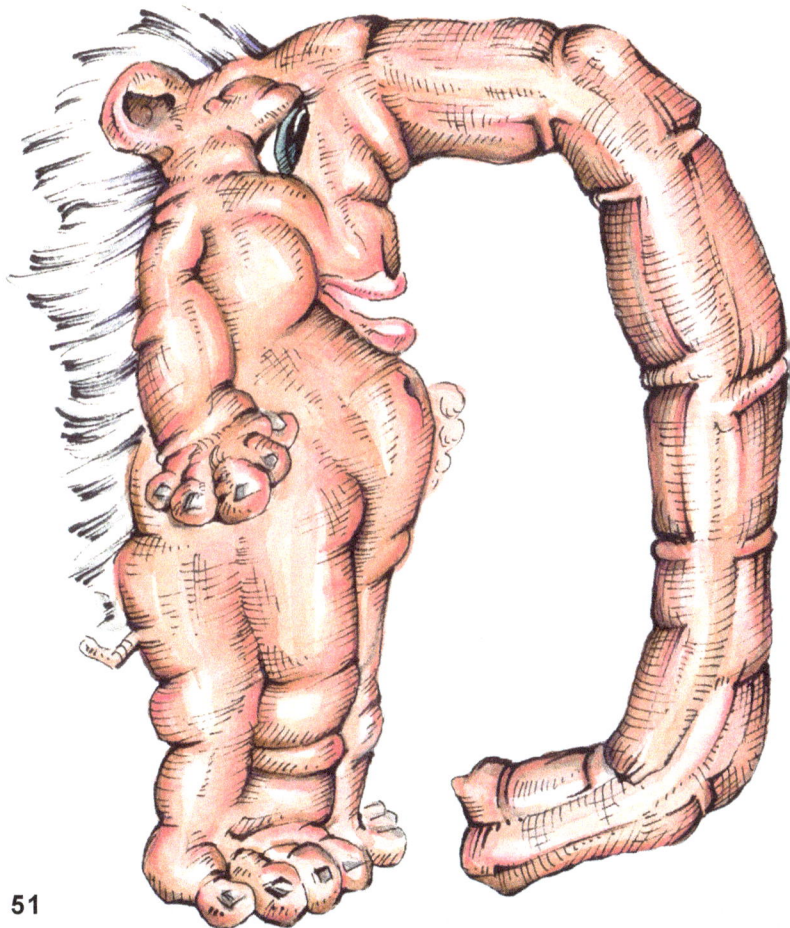

51

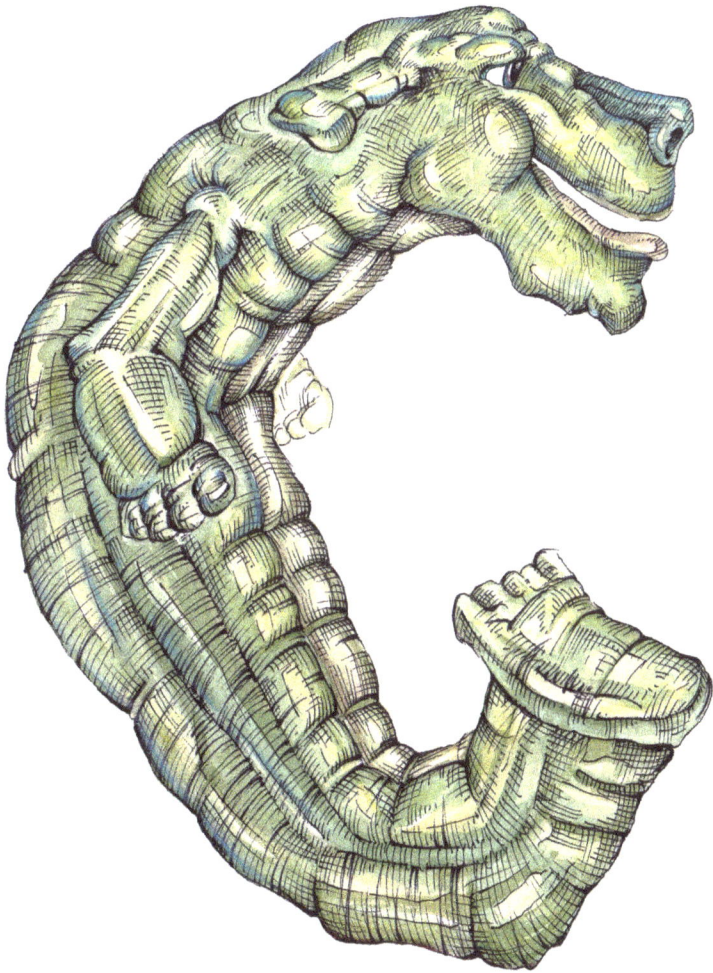
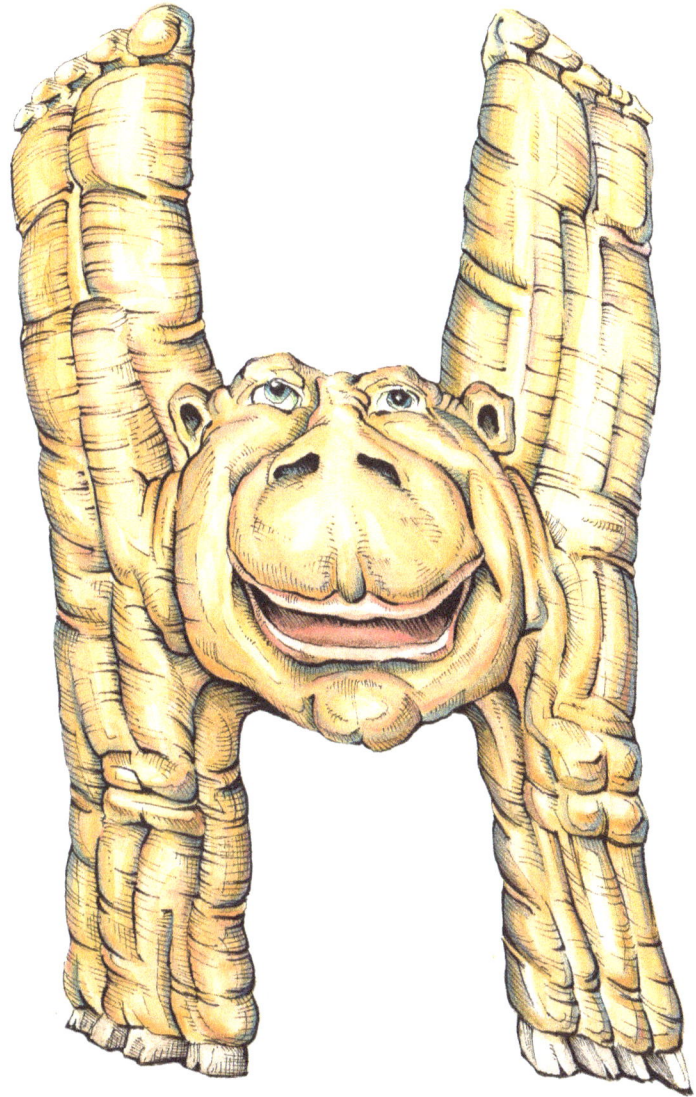

57

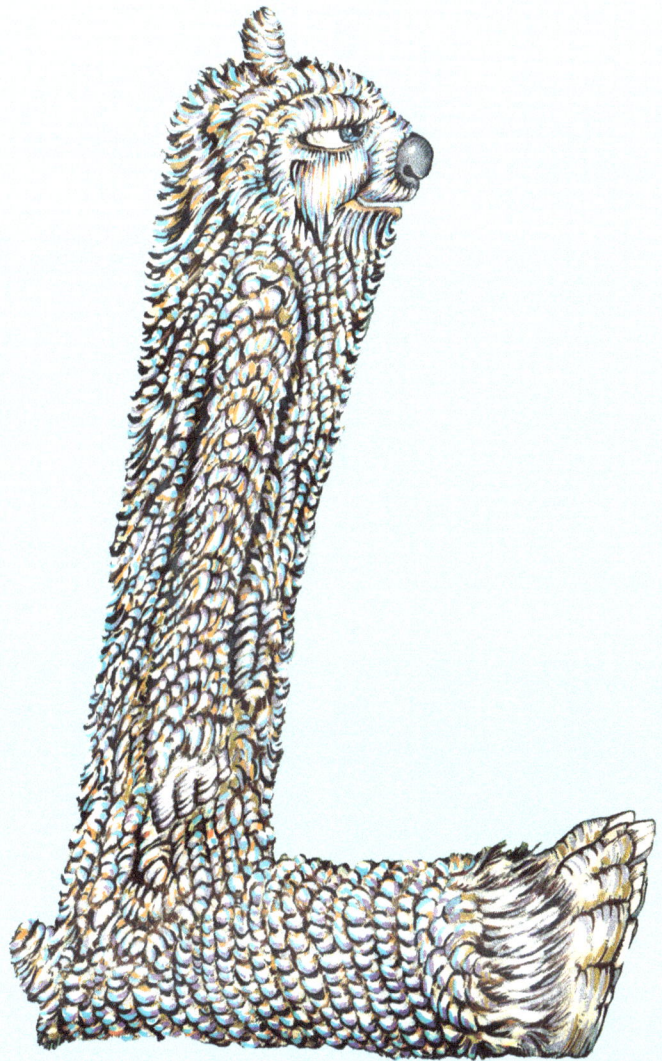

59

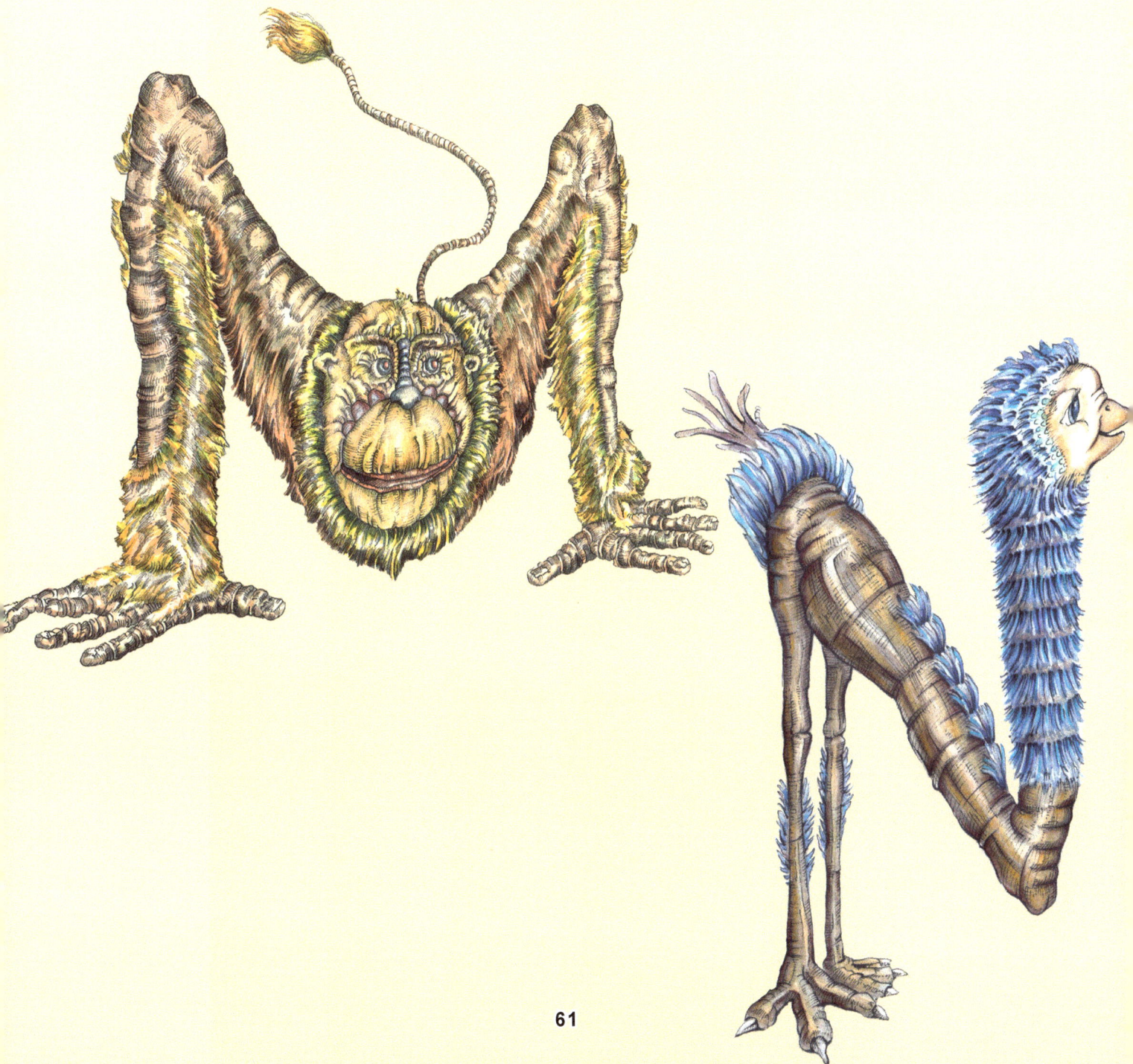

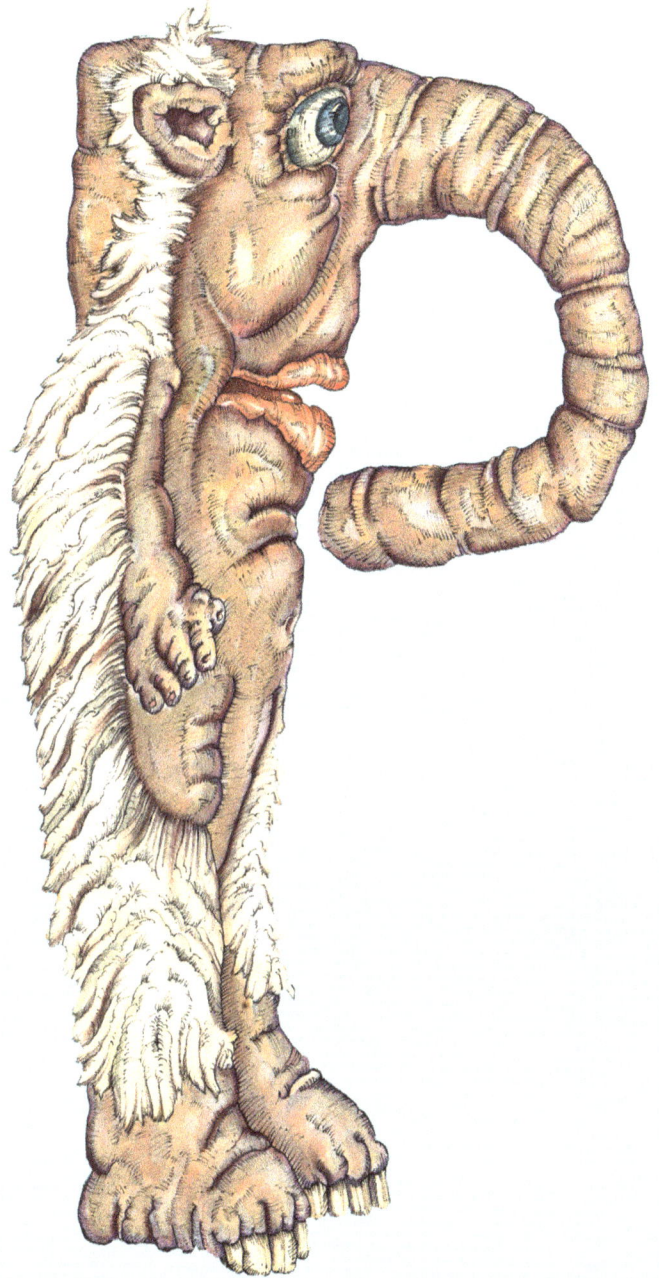

63

69

71

73

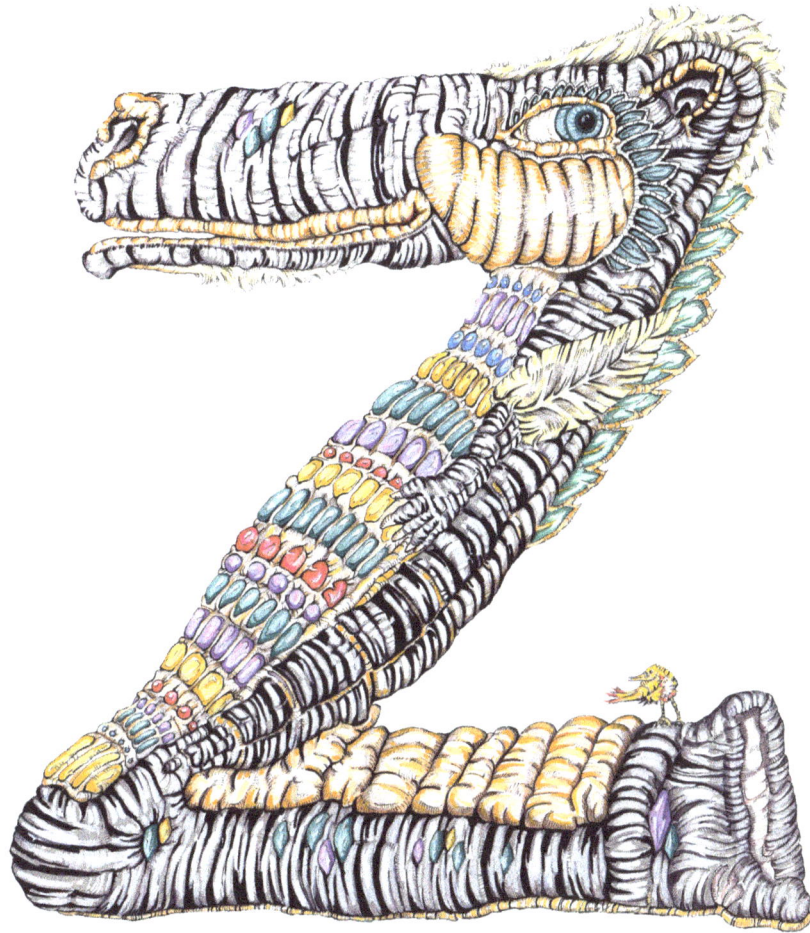

Epilogue:

a living alphabet - the final story

'The Great Weaver of Words' guided the alphabet creatures until they found the humans. These were some of the first humans on planet earth, a small clutch of Homo sapiens lead by a giant couple, Curfeu and Curflex. In time, these emerging humans found connection with the furry, feathery and robust creatures sent by the 'Weaver'.

Our living alphabet settled close to the enclave of Curfeu and Curflex. Each night singing and dancing to their letter sounds as all the humans gathered around. The humans clever as they are imitated the creature's sounds discovering they too wanted to dance - dance around and around. They made drawings in the sand, carved the creature's shapes into trees and Curfew made large replicas of each of the twenty six with gathered stones. His love for them had become so great.

Would that this story ended here, but it goes on into darker realms. All did not go as planned for the creatures even under the protection of the Great Weaver. Earth was a young planet and a great prize for any entity within our galaxy or beyond that could occupy our planet with their own language; they're very own alphabet. So it was, a comet sent from a remote exoplanet in the chromium galaxy many light years from planet earth arrived; within, an evil alphabet lead by the terrifying figure of Argoil the evil A.. They had one purpose - to destroy the living alphabet and rule the tongues of the emerging humans.

War ensued between the small human community and the malevolent invading creatures. Our living alphabet was caught between the two, and none of them were adept at defending themselves; they fought valiantly but were overwhelmed by Argoil and his creature's dark determination. They all perished. Curfeu and Curflex managed to drive Argoil's band out, beyond the limits of their known world. However they never forgot their singing, dancing creature friends; nor did Argoil cease in his determination to infect the future of human speech.

Meanwhile, the Great Weaver of words gathered the living alphabet 'in spirit' asking each one to be a guide to its own letter form as the humans multiply and create ever so many languages. "Touch peoples hearts with your letter shape and sound, enliven their love for the beauty within their Words".

So it became, the great struggle with Words. When one feels delight in a letter or a word, it's possible that the Weaver's creatures are somewhere about – attempting to touch your heart with the beauty of letters and the power of Words.

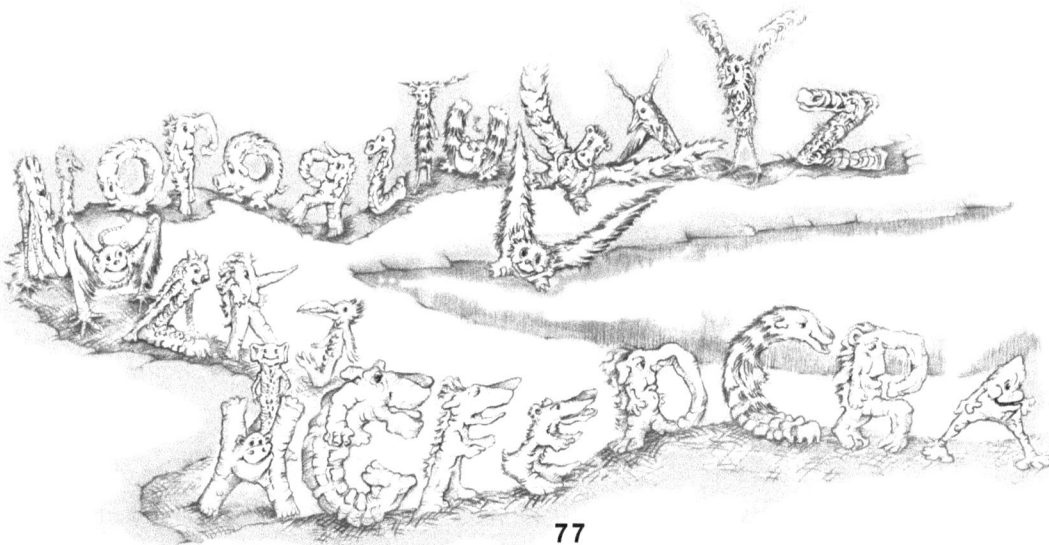

www.ingramcontent.com/pod-product-compliance
Lightning Source LLC
Chambersburg PA
CBHW042340030426
42335CB00030B/3417